Information Systems Engineering Library

Improving the Maintainability of Software

Richard West

CCTA

November 1993

LONDON: HMSO

© Crown Copyright 1993

Applications for reproduction should be made to HMSO

First published 1993

ISBN 0 11 330585 0

For further information regarding this publication and other CCTA products please contact:

CCTA Library
Riverwalk House
157-161 Millbank
London SW1P 4RT

071-217-3331

Contents

Foreword

Acknowledgements

1 Introduction   1

    1.1   Background

    1.2   Purpose

    1.3   Who should read this volume

    1.4   Derivation of guidance

    1.5   Structure of the volume

2 Overview   5

3 What is maintainability?   7

    3.1   Definitions

    3.2   Importance of maintainability

    3.3   Maintainability and the software lifecycle

    3.4   Factors affecting maintainability

4 Developing maintainable software systems   17

    4.1   Planning for maintainability

    4.2   Analysis considerations

    4.3   Design considerations

    4.4   Build considerations

    4.5   The test environment

    4.6   Documentation

    4.7   Adherence to standards and methods

    4.8   Maintainability and quality

5	**Preserving and improving the maintainability of software**		**35**
	5.1	Introduction	
	5.2	Maintainability objectives	
	5.3	Corrective maintenance	
	5.4	Perfective maintenance	
	5.5	Adaptive maintenance	
	5.6	Preventive maintenance	
	5.7	Maintenance staff	
6	**Monitoring software maintainability**		**45**
	6.1	The need to measure	
	6.2	Assessing software maintainability	
	6.3	Assessment results	
	6.4	Objectives and actions	
	6.5	Reaping the benefits	

Annexes   **53**

   A Maintainability measure

   B Maintainability index

   C Example maintainability plans

   D The process and activities of software maintenance

Bibliography   **95**

Glossary   **99**

Foreword

The **Information Systems Engineering Library** provides guidance on managing and carrying out Information Systems Engineering activities. In the IS life cycle, Information Systems Engineering takes place once the IS strategy has been defined. It is concerned with the development and ongoing improvement of information systems up to the operational stage, when systems become the responsibility of infrastructure management.

The Information Systems Engineering Library builds on guidance in the CCTA IS Guides, particularly set A: *Management and Planning Set* and set B: *Systems Development Set* and complements other CCTA products, in particular the project management method, PRINCE, and the systems analysis and design method, SSADM.

Volumes in the Information Systems Engineering Library are of interest to varying levels of staff from IS directors to IS providers, helping them to improve the quality and productivity of their IS development work. Some volumes in this library should also be of interest to business managers, IS users and those involved in market testing, whose business operations depend on having effective IS support by means of Information Systems Engineering activities.

The Information Systems Engineering Library also complements other related CCTA publications, particularly the IT Infrastructure Library for operational issues and the IS Planning Subject Guides for strategic issues.

CCTA welcomes customer views on Information Systems Engineering Library publications. Please send your comments to:

> Customer Services
> Information Systems Engineering Group
> Gildengate House
> Upper Green Lane
> NORWICH
> NR3 1DW

Acknowledgements

The assistance of Hilary Calow, Anne Kirby and Julia Hollings of FI Group under contract to CCTA is gratefully acknowledged.

1 Introduction

1.1 Background

Much of today's business, both government and private sector, depends, among other things, on the reliability of software. This software must be maintained to take account of changes in business requirements or to correct errors. Because this maintenance is expensive and time-consuming, it is clearly desirable to have a software system design which places as few demands on the maintainer as possible.

Many of the problems experienced in maintaining existing software systems stem from the fact that these systems have poor maintainability characteristics. This affects not only the quality of the software itself, but also the quality of the business application supported by that software.

The maintenance phase of a software system is usually longer than the development phase and, typically, accounts for two thirds of a system's lifecycle cost. Furthermore, maintenance is mainly a reactive process which often has to be completed within tight timescales, and any actions which lead to greater efficiency or reduce the necessity for maintenance are to be welcomed.

There is, therefore, a need to develop new software which can be maintained easily and effectively. Similarly, it is necessary to preserve and where necessary improve the maintainability of existing software.

1.2 Purpose

The purpose of this volume is to provide practical guidance on the maintainability of software. The volume:

- defines maintainability and explains why it is important

- describes the factors which contribute to the maintainability of software under development and of existing software systems

- gives guidance on building for and improving maintainability

- provides a simple approach for assessing maintainability.

1.3 Who should read this volume

This volume is aimed at:

- project managers and software developers

- managers responsible for the maintenance of application software

- staff responsible for writing new software or maintaining existing software

- managers who purchase new software from a third party, or are responsible for contracting out software maintenance.

1.4 Derivation of guidance

The guidance given in this volume draws on the results of a study carried out on behalf of CCTA, the aim of which was to identify factors which affect maintainability and to assess their relative importance. A strongly practical approach was adopted, and information was gathered on 35 current application software systems from eight organisations in the following business sectors:

- central government

- life assurance

- credit card processing
- retail accounting
- research and development.

In six out of the eight organisations, application maintenance support was provided by a third party supplier.

Mainframe, PC and distributed systems were included in the study, covering both batch and on-line processing systems. However, no defence, command and control or safety critical systems were examined.

Systems maintenance staff provided information on the maintainability factors which they considered to be important, and detailed questionnaires were then completed for the chosen systems providing information on maintainability factors and current activity. The relative maintainability of these systems was assessed by reference to data on the extent and success of recent maintenance activity. Statistical analyses of this data highlighted the factors which had the greatest impact on the maintainability of the systems.

The conclusions of the study, together with current best practice and material from other sources, provides a strong practical basis for the guidance given in this volume.

| 1.5 | **Structure of the volume** |

This volume is divided into six chapters and four Annexes. Following this introductory chapter, the volume is arranged as follows:

Chapter 2 is an overview of the volume and is essential reading.

Chapter 3 defines what is meant by maintainability and examines the factors affecting it. This chapter is also essential reading.

Chapter 4 explains how to produce maintainable software systems. It is of particular interest to developers of new software and those purchasing development services from third parties.

Chapter 5 explains how to preserve and improve the maintainability of existing software systems. It is of particular interest to software maintainers, including purchasers of maintenance services from third parties.

Chapter 6 describes an approach to assess and monitor software maintainability, both quantitatively and qualitatively. It is of interest to developers and maintainers and those purchasing development or maintenance services. The chapter explains how to interpret the results obtained using Annexes A, B and D.

Annex A describes the approach used to assess factors which contribute to the software maintainability measure. It provides a form which can be used to gather data for the maintainability factor assessment.

Annex B explains how to derive the maintainability index.

Annex C provides example maintainability plans referred to in Chapter 4.

Annex D provides information on the process and activities of software maintenance, which may be utilised when preparing action plans following maintainability assessment.

The Bibliography lists all the publications referenced, together with additional material which readers may find of value.

The Glossary defines the terms used in the volume.

2   Overview

A software system which is easily maintainable is most likely to deliver the results the business requires, and will be amenable to change. Its maintenance is likely to be faster, less error prone and less costly than a system with poor maintainability. This volume provides a definition of maintainability and examines some of the important factors which contribute to it.

Maintainability must be planned, designed and implemented at every stage in the system lifecycle. Expedients to save time or money during development can all too often lead to significant increase in the risk of error and cost of future maintenance. The volume describes the factors to consider in producing new software so that it is easily maintained; it also describes how to preserve and improve the maintainability of existing software.

Purchasers of software need to be aware that the cost of future software maintenance should be included in the business case for purchase. Poorly designed software will increase maintenance cost and strain the resources of the business. Similarly, purchasers of maintenance services must recognise that software which has been poorly designed or maintained will be likely to increase the service cost.

Managers responsible for software systems should assess the software's maintainability periodically (perhaps once every six months), noting any significant change in performance. If the business is planning to contract out maintenance work, it is worthwhile running a check beforehand to establish a baseline against which future performance of the application software system or maintainer can be measured.

Much research has been carried out into the consequences of software attributes on software maintenance, and source code attributes are often considered to the exclusion of everything else. However, there are other important features which must be measured and assessed for their impact on maintainability. This volume considers software system, process and environmental factors; it explores their importance and describes a simple approach for assessing maintainability.

The success of a software system is governed by development and maintenance processes; all components are influenced by their environmental factors, as shown in Figure 1.

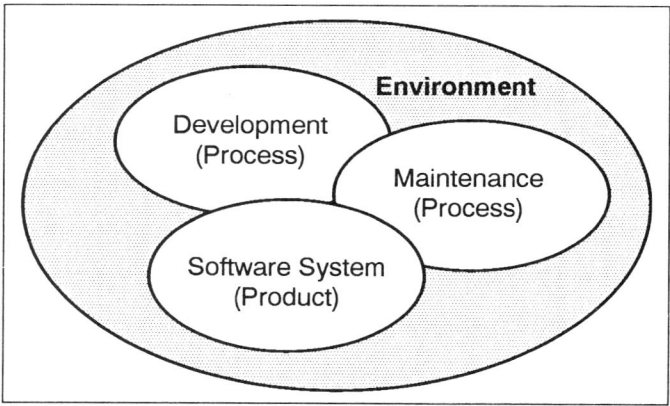

Figure 1: Maintainability as a concept

The volume describes how to interpret the results of maintainability assessment and how to prioritise those actions required to improve maintainability.

3 What is maintainability?

3.1 Definitions

Software maintainability is an attribute of a program or software system. Schneidewind (1987) defines this as:

> *"The ease with which a software system can be corrected when errors or deficiencies occur and can be expanded, modified or contracted to satisfy new requirements."*

Software maintainability affects maintenance itself, which the IEEE defines as:

> *"Any modification of a software product after delivery, to correct faults, to improve performance or other attributes or to adapt the product to a changed environment."*

Using this definition, major changes to a software system (often thought of as development), should be regarded as maintenance. The ease with which such changes can be implemented is affected by the maintainability of the software. For the purposes of this volume, a software system or product includes:

- source and object code, application programs, procedures, rules and objects
- job control language (JCL) statements
- database and screen definitions
- documentation covering the nature and use of the software system
- test material.

The operational performance of a software system, including response time and throughputs, is affected by the data, the operational environment and the people who use and operate the system. These elements may also be regarded as part of the total system.

Maintainability is concerned with the whole software system throughout its entire life span. The way in which its various constituents affect maintainability is examined in later chapters.

3.2 Importance of maintainability

The quality of information systems has a profound effect on the businesses which use them. Maintainability is one aspect of quality and it affects the cost of IS support to business. Systems *must* be maintainable if they are to support business effectively.

Software systems with good maintainability have the following advantages over those with poor maintainability:

- the software is easier and quicker to change and therefore the system is more cost effective to maintain

- changes are less likely to introduce error

- the software has a longer useful lifetime

- the software system is more likely to deliver a better return on investment.

By contrast, a system with poor maintainability has the following undesirable characteristics:

- more resources are required for maintenance and, consequently, poor maintainability adversely affects the IS budget

- the software is difficult to change, and a backlog of work may build up causing delay and inhibiting changes required by the business

- there may be more operational problems, a higher rate of system failure and more lost working time, or even damage to business as a result of continuing software problems

- any changes are themselves more likely to contain errors

- the expected return on investment may be reduced.

3.3 Maintainability and the software lifecycle

The software lifecycle is a representation of the complete lifetime of a software system from conception to decommissioning. Typically, some two-thirds of a system's lifecycle cost is spent on maintenance. Because prevention is better than cure, it is important to design for good maintainability at the outset.

Choices made early in the lifecycle may have far-reaching implications for maintenance at later stages. For example, during development there may be pressure to meet a particularly tight deadline, and this may be regarded as more important than taking the additional time to produce a system with good modularity and well annotated source code. However, a modular system written in readily understandable code will be easier to maintain; it may, therefore, contribute more to reducing the overall business cost than meeting the pre-determined development deadline.

Software maintenance is an activity in its own right. Consequently, the responsibility of the maintenance team should be clearly defined and maintenance work should not be regarded as merely an offshoot of development.

Managers of development and maintenance staff, including those responsible for managing the provision of development or maintenance services by third parties, have a key role to play. Once they have recognised the importance of maintainability, they should ensure that this is incorporated at all stages in the lifecycle of the system. Maintainability features should be designed into the software system during development; during subsequent maintenance, they should be preserved and, where justified by business need, improved.

Development and maintenance processes are both controlled by a management process concerned with planning and monitoring, control of risk, costs and quality.

Figure 2 is taken from the ISE Library volume: *Management of Software Maintenance* and shows the maintenance lifecycle relative to development stages.

Major and minor maintenance projects are shown, including stages equivalent to those for a new development project. They are:

- initiation and cost benefit analysis
- requirements analysis specification
- logical systems specification
- physical design
- development
- user trials
- release control
- post implementation review and benefit evaluation.

Minor maintenance projects are those under a set cost, size and risk limit, with an evaluation of the existing system showing that no change of the basic design is required.

Chapter 3
What is maintainability?

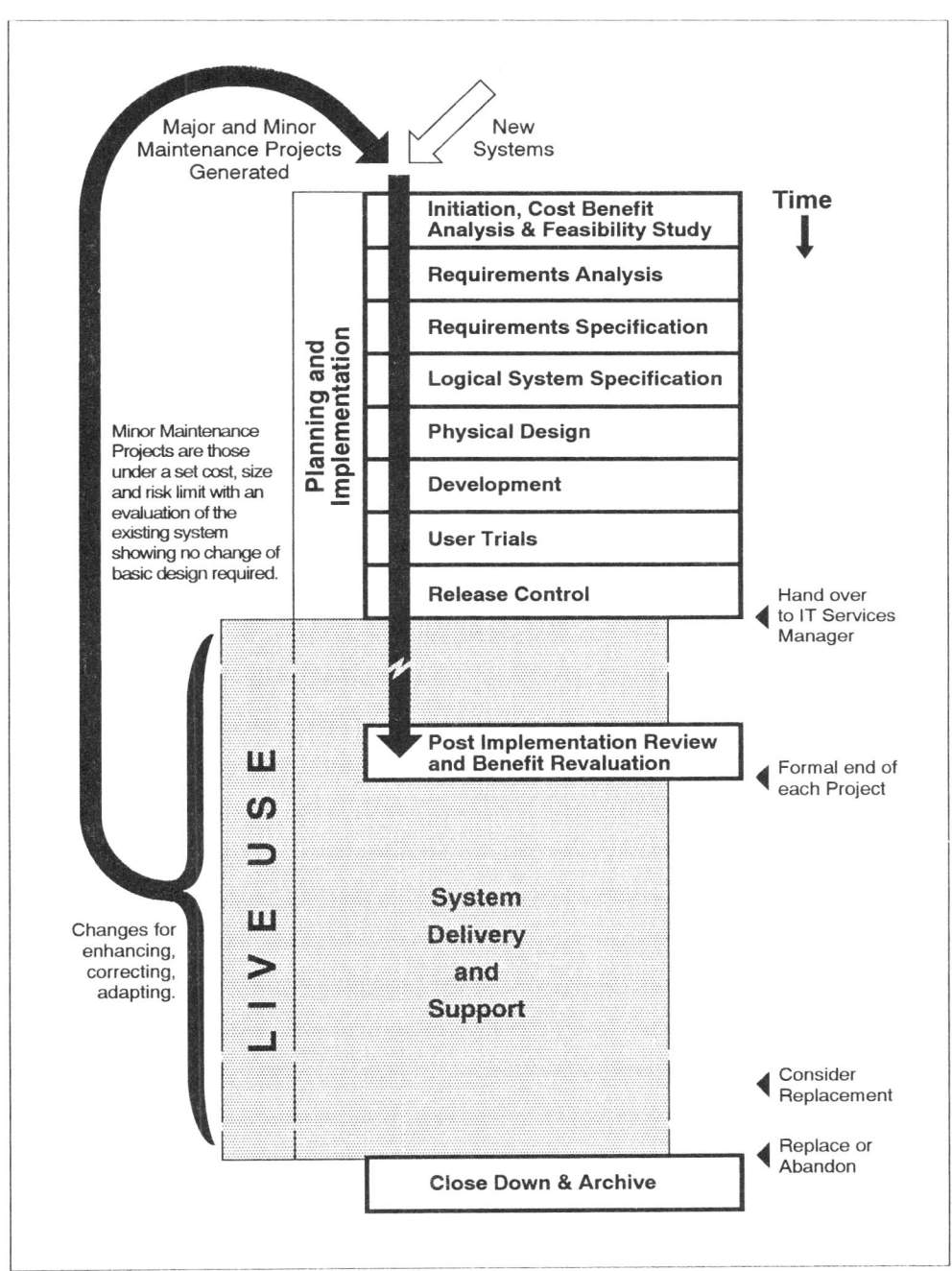

Figure 2: Maintenance in the IS project lifecycle

3.3.1 CCTA methods

It is easier to build maintainability into all aspects of the software lifecycle if an inter-linked set of IS development and management methods is used, such as SSADM, PRINCE and CRAMM.

- SSADM is the CCTA method for analysis and design of information systems

- PRINCE is the CCTA method for project management

- CRAMM is the CCTA risk analysis and design methodology.

The PRINCE project board for an IS development project should stipulate the maintainability requirements of the delivered system. The project assurance team should check maintainability goals and measurement throughout development, and measure maintainability at the post implementation review. The IS organisation should ensure that it is monitored thereafter. The project and stage managers should plan for maintainability in all project deliverables and ensure that timescales and objectives are realistic. The quality control process must include an assessment of maintainability in all quality reviews.

Whenever IS project risk is analysed, the standard CRAMM approach should be augmented to include an assessment of the business risk of poor or reduced maintainability which adversely affects the ability to implement necessary changes effectively and efficiently.

3.3.2 Development

Development of a new software system involves five steps:

1. an analysis of requirements; these should be defined as clearly as possible at the outset, or the development team may find itself maintaining the system and making corrections to the software before it has been used

Chapter 3
What is maintainability?

2 production of a sound design which incorporates the requirements in the most efficient and cost effective way

3 building an accurate and efficient implementation of the design

4 testing to validate that all requirements are met in the implementation

5 implementation.

Maintainability has to be built in at each step in this sequence. These steps may be incorporated into software development in different ways depending on the lifecycle model chosen; different types of projects need different models. The IT Infrastructure Library volume: *Software Lifecycle Support* discusses several possible lifecycle models. Chapter 4 of this volume examines development issues in more detail.

3.3.3 Maintenance

Software maintenance consists of five steps:

1 understanding the problem or requirement for change

2 identifying and describing the changes to be made to the system

3 making the changes

4 testing the changed software, and regression testing

5 implementing the upgraded system and assessing the entire system at the post implementation review.

Future maintainability has to be considered at each of these steps and current maintainability affects the execution of the steps.

Improving the Maintainability of Software

Chapter 5 examines maintenance issues in more detail. The Information Systems Engineering Library volume: *Management of Software Maintenance* provides guidance on the management of software maintenance.

3.4 Factors affecting maintainability

The overall maintainability of a software system depends on three interacting groups of factors, summarised in Figure 1.

Figure 3 shows some of the factors that were found in the CCTA study, to influence the overall maintainability of a software system. Definitions of the terms used are included in Annex A.

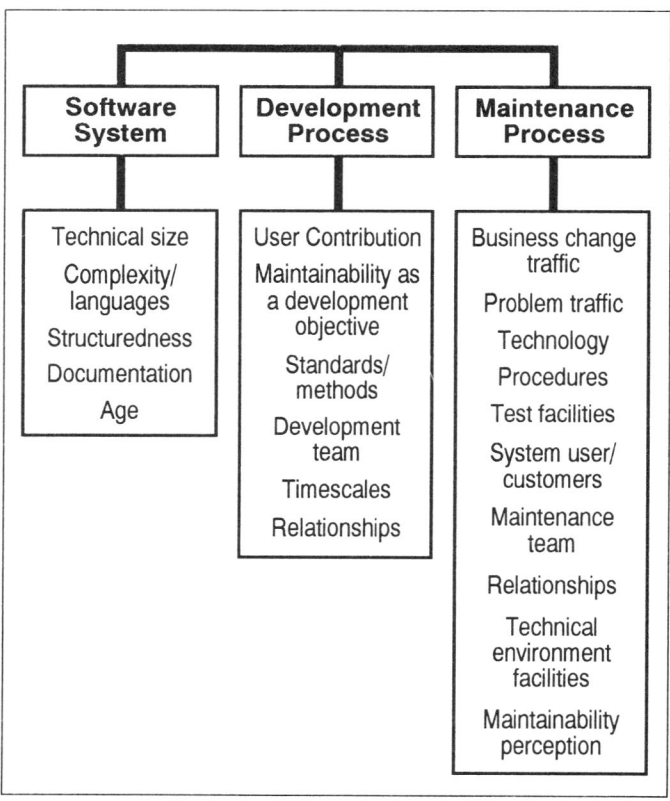

Figure 3: Important maintainability factors

Chapter 3
What is maintainability?

Most factors are open to improvement, though some may require substantial effort, especially if a software system's maintainability has been neglected over several years. Variables such as age are not improvable, and factors specific to the development phase are not improvable during maintenance. Whether or not they can be improved on, factors can be assessed for their relative importance to maintainability. For example, development timescales have less impact than adequate documentation; but how much less and how do they compare to the use of good testing facilities? Annex A describes the relative importance of the maintainability factors and their constituent parts.

The factors listed below were found in the CCTA study to be the most important:

- completeness and usefulness of the program descriptions

- the extent to which the system is structured into modules

- the interpersonal skills of the maintenance team and their ability to work well with others

- the average module size

- the use of parameters

- the complexity of the business function for which the software system was designed

- the technical complexity of the software system

- the level of management commitment to the software maintenance function as perceived by the maintenance team.

These factors should be considered by both developers and maintainers.

4 Developing maintainable software systems

Software maintainability should always be made an explicit development objective. Experience shows that where software maintainability is set as a key objective, the resulting product is more maintainable.

Improved software maintainability may also be achieved implicitly as a consequence of meeting other objectives. For example, a decision to parameterise variables which may change during the life of a software system will be likely to improve maintainability. Software maintainability must be designed into the software system at the point when the cost of doing so is smallest and the resulting benefits are large. Building in software maintainability at early stages of development, also helps when developers have to apply a system change before implementation.

4.1 Planning for maintainability

Maintainability should be included in the business case for the development or purchase of new software. It is an appropriate development objective because it will increase the value of the system to the business. Software systems which are easier to maintain require fewer resources to facilitate business change. A high level of maintainability will also limit the risk of software failure and make it possible to achieve faster restoration of services after any failure has occurred. This is of particular value where system failure means business failure.

Development managers should produce a maintainability plan for software under development. The plan should set out maintainability objectives and goals for both the development and maintenance phases of the system lifecycle. Customers are likely to have to pay directly for software maintenance effort, computer time and other resources, and therefore they should be involved in setting maintainability objectives.

Consequently, the plan should be produced in consultation with the system customers and any deviations from the plan should be agreed, recorded and monitored. Example plans are given in Annex C.

There are several ways to express maintainability objectives, for example:

- a target cost of maintenance

- level of resources required for maintenance

- error density and stability of the software system

- speed and accuracy of implementing change.

Setting maintainability objectives should also contribute to the return on investment calculation. During software development stages many organisations do not think about the cost of maintaining a software system or estimate the resources required. If software maintainability objectives are agreed and acted upon during development, the costs and resources required for maintenance can be reduced and predicted more accurately. If the necessary data is available, predictions can be based on the experience of maintaining other similar systems whose maintainability has been assessed and, perhaps, improved as outlined in Section 6.

To be effective, maintainability plans should address the following factors:

- the size of the programs within the system

- the extent to which the system is modular, parameterised and comprehensible

- the completeness and accuracy of the documentation

- customer/user involvement in the development process

- adherence to standards and methods for the development process

- development team skills, experience, business knowledge, motivation and attitude to the development work

- development timescales

- relationships/communications between various groups involved in the development of the system

- the test facilities in use.

These factors are examined more closely in Annex A.

Other factors should not be ignored, however, and the development team should always be kept abreast of all the specified maintainability objectives. Members of the development team should be involved in setting objectives, and the team should be provided with the support, commitment and resources required to meet them.

Software obtained from third party suppliers should be maintainable. Purchasers should insist on the inclusion of maintainability objectives in the development plan and ensure that these objectives are measurable. Systems with high visibility, such as management support tools or executive information systems, or systems directly affecting the public, must be easy to use and be quickly correctable. In such cases any extra expenditure incurred on providing good maintainability may be more readily accepted.

The following sections of this chapter explore the factors which help in the development of maintainable software as they apply to the various stages of systems development.

- sections 4.2 - 4.4 cover analysis, design and build

- section 4.5 covers the test environment

- section 4.6 describes the maintainers' need for system documentation

- sections 4.7 and 4.8 describe the links between maintainability and development standards and methods, also between maintainability and quality.

4.2 Analysis considerations

Requirement Analysis considerations should include:

- the likely type and degree of future enhancement needed

- the acceptable levels of problem traffic

- functional complexity of the software system and the business application it supports

- the likely frequency and type of technical environment changes.

The likely amount of future enhancement work should be considered explicitly at the analysis stage. The amount can often be predicted from the expected changes in business function or working arrangements, and from examining the history of existing comparable systems.

The aim is to build a software system which will accommodate the most change with the least effort over the longest time. Any anticipated business and technology changes can be incorporated into the functional requirements or facilitated for the future. The use of parameters is an important factor in producing maintainable systems, and analysts should carefully identify situations where this approach would be beneficial when obtaining user requirements.

The volume of problem traffic should be considered by assessing:

- the likely levels of corrective maintenance
- the types of error which may arise.

The levels of quality control and testing activities should be set accordingly. For example:

- providing a parameter to make a future change of function easier may require increased testing
- including more than one test plan, walk-through or inspection to cater for each item in the quality plan will reduce future errors by increasing the quality of testing.

The functional complexity of the software system affects its subsequent maintainability and should be reduced if possible. Documentation should be initiated at the analysis stage and should include a description of the business application of the system. The standards of documentation should remain high throughout the development phase and beyond.

4.3 Design considerations

Maintainability is affected by design decisions, including:

- data structures
- language
- structuredness
- distributed systems
- packaged software
- operating environment.

Designing for maintainability is also designing for *testability* and *flexibility*. These concepts should be considered together at the Design Stage. Further information may be found in the IT Infrastructure Library volume: *Testing an IT Service for Operational Use*, and in the Information Systems Engineering Library volume *Management of Software Maintenance*.

All design decisions should be recorded in the system documentation, which should indicate the alternatives considered and the reasons for their selection or rejection.

4.3.1 Data structures

Data structures should be kept as simple as possible and easy to understand. Using structured data analysis techniques, such as Relational Data Analysis, produces a well-structured logical data design.

Design implementation (physical design) should take maintainability into account. Those responsible should:

- keep physical data structures in line with logical data views
- use flat or hierarchical structures in preference to networks where this is consistent with acceptable efficient performance of system functions
- minimise the number of hierarchical levels

- minimise linkages between files (unless absolutely necessary to reduce data storage needs)

- use a data dictionary system wherever possible, especially when using a DBMS.

The use of CASE tools can be highly beneficial in development and maintenance. These often provide a means of producing good data documentation which can be maintained easily.

4.3.2 Language

A system constructed in several languages is hard to maintain, as is one written in a language unfamiliar to the maintainers.

The long term implications of using a given language should be considered at the outset. This should include factors such as the supplier's commitment to the language compiler or any support tool used, support for it and the availability of personnel skilled in the use of the language. Use of language compilers which conform to the appropriate ISO standard is recommended, especially where system portability is a current or possible requirement.

Systems developed using 4GLs may prove to be highly maintainable, particularly where all anticipated changes can be achieved by simple alterations to a few parameters. However, the use of 4GLs can reduce maintainability where there is an inherent lack of programmer control over the execution process, and where programmer intervention is inhibited. Although the latter point may be regarded as advantageous because it limits tinkering with the source code, it could result in a substantial amount of work to implement a relatively small change, resulting in increased cost and time. In some cases there is a lack of tools, particularly to aid debugging, which affects maintainability. This can be exacerbated where there is difficulty in adding diagnostics for debugging. Before choosing a 4GL for a given application it is, therefore, necessary to consider not only the requirements of the initial application, but also the nature of the changes which may have to be implemented during the life of the system.

The portability of a 4GL should also be considered if it is anticipated that there will be a significant change in the hardware/software operating environment during the life of the application software system.

4.3.3 Structuredness

The objective is to produce a system which is easily navigable, is well organised in simple modules with few interfaces and with minimised complexity. Important features are:

- the structuredness of the code (code organisation must be easy to follow and understand)

- the size of the modules (smaller modules are easier to maintain)

- the modularity of the design (each module should have a clear function)

- the use of parameters (the aim is to be able to vary system function without the need for a software change)

- the interfaces between the modules and other systems must be clear and well documented.

Structured programs are easier to understand and change.

4.3.4 Distributed systems

Software systems implemented on more than one platform, or with distributed components, often require more time to implement and change than non-distributed systems. However, careful design can improve maintainability, for example, by adopting a client/server structure in which the server application is self contained.

Portability can be improved by strict adherence to standards in languages and interfaces. Possible adverse effects of non-adherence to approved standards should be taken into account before finalising any decision to deviate from these. Any deviation from standards must be carefully recorded and the reasons for such action clearly set out.

4.3.5 Packaged software

Although packaged software systems may be simple and inexpensive to implement, they can present problems during the maintenance phase if changes necessitated by a business change cannot be fully implemented. There are several factors which affect this, including a lack of flexibility in the package, errors contained in the package, non-availability of source code, limited documentation and the requirement to keep up with new releases. When selecting a package, the following considerations should be included in the checklist:

- the skill required to support and maintain the package

- the number and frequency of releases and the ease of installation and acceptance testing

- the level of customisation needed and the impact of this on release implementation and maintenance.

Customisation should be minimised and avoided where possible, apart from that inherent in the package design and necessary for installation, such as the use of parameters. In general, the aim is to have the supplier maintain the package software.

It is even more important to avoid customisation of systems software as this will impact all other systems run under that software and probably void supplier's support obligations.

4.3.6 Operating environment

Decisions are taken during the design stage which influence the operational aspects of the live system and impact its maintainability. Facilities in the operating environment are needed to help maintainers respond to crises, such as system failure, and quickly restore system function. All emergency action should be followed by the approved maintenance procedures, and techniques to correct errors and preserve maintainability.

Particular consideration should be given to the following facilities and features required of the operating environment:

- Controlled access to live data for software maintainers (where this would not breach security)

- the ease with which problems can be simulated or reproduced

- the availability of editors, debugging and impact analysis tools

- quick and easy backup, recovery and restart facilities, including transaction logging and audit trails

- resilience of the software system to failure

- good response time for system users, for example, less than four seconds

- software system performance, with regard to the installation and business users' requirements

- facilities for increased capacity and improved performance.

These considerations may influence the way in which system changes can be made. For example, a change to the size of a data item may create operational problems, and maintainability may be frustrated because extra disc space is needed and cannot be accommodated or provided.

Additionally, consideration should be given to the usability of the end product of a system, which will have an impact on maintainability. If users find a system difficult to understand and operate, or if the performance is poor, they will tend to make more mistakes or not use the system efficiently. Both these conditions will generate change requests in the future.

Chapter 4
Developing maintainable software systems

The IT Infrastructure Library volume: *Testing an IT Service for Operational Use* covers usability testing.

4.4 Build considerations

During the build stage of a software system, consideration should be given to the size, complexity and structure of the programs. Software should be built from well defined building blocks.

A module should execute a logical function, or a set of functions which have clear boundaries. Code which is common to more than one logical strand of processing should be written in separate modules. It is not helpful to specify a precise size for a module. The ideal is that modules should be small enough to be understood, modified and tested easily. However, if they are too small, then this merely transfers the complexity of the system up to the next level, where, arguably, it is even harder for the maintainer to understand what is happening. A module hierarchy chart must always be produced showing, for each module, all the points in the system from where it is called, all the modules called by it and stating briefly the function of the module.

There are several well-tried approaches for assessing complexity of code. This volume does not discuss code complexity in detail, as this is already covered in existing publications (see Bibliography).

If organisations do not currently have recommended standards for writing code, then it is strongly recommended that urgent consideration is given to this subject. Good installation standards for code will contribute to the overall quality of the software and simplify the task of the software maintainer.

The more predictable the style and structure of code, the less time will have to be spent in understanding the individual approach of the original programmer, or (as is more likely) the individuality of the various people who have amended the code over the years. Writing well-structured code to an approved standard will serve to remove unnecessary complexity from programs and modules.

The use of CASE tools to generate source code may achieve the twin objectives of speeding up system development and providing the maintainers with a more easily understood view of the system when changes have to be implemented.

Reuse of software components is also to be encouraged as widely as practicable in order to increase software quality and reliability, improve development productivity and reduce lifecycle costs.

Accessible libraries of 'certified' reusable code components performing standard functions such as error checking and date calculations, are widespread. Developers should both reuse existing code and develop new code with reuse in mind.

Guidelines covering all of the above must be produced for the developers by the managers responsible for development, and all standards must be clearly documented and understood. Developers must:

- adhere to agreed technical standards and codes of practice

- ensure code, documentation, charts and test plans are all readable and easily understood

- produce documentation to agreed standards and ensure that it is current when the system is implemented

- ensure consistent use of naming conventions.

Tools exist which can aid in the quality assurance and control of these factors.

Programs should be easy to understand and change. The code should be structured, annotated and should conform to technical standards.

4.5 The test environment

A carefully designed test environment is essential. If changes to the implemented software are poorly tested, errors may be overlooked which will cause subsequent system failure. A good test environment helps improve the quality of testing and preserves the system's quality and maintainability. The test environment should include the appropriate tests and provide support for future maintenance. The test environment must include a testbed containing valid and invalid data. There must be a facility to add further data, and amend the existing data. Well structured test environments and documentation will also assist in the extent to which use can be made of automatic testing aids, particularly for regression testing.

A test harness optimises the usefulness of a testbed, providing a simplified way of running tests and checking data. During systems development, tests should be created and incorporated into the test environment to check known or likely error conditions. All tests must be repeatable. Further error conditions may be found as changes are made to the system, and the test environment should be kept in step with the live environment so that any change to the use of a system is incorporated in the tests.

Testing facilities are particularly important when correcting errors in the implemented software; problems in the live system need to be simulated quickly and their solutions thoroughly tested for accuracy. A good test environment includes an interactive support tool for test running, which will enable the maintainer to control a test run and monitor the extent to which the test data has exercised the code being tested. Some reverse engineering tools also provide help with testing.

All test facilities must be documented so that they are easily understood and used. Equally, the test facilities must be kept up-to-date to reflect changes to the systems that are the subject of testing.

Integration and regression testing can be time-consuming and expensive components of the maintenance process, especially in environments where systems are tightly integrated. Consideration should be given to setting up an independent test facility to carry out these functions. This could add to the annual cost of carrying out software maintenance but will help to minimise errors in the live system, thus providing an overall benefit. It will be for each organisation to decide on the most appropriate approach to testing, in order to ensure the highest quality of software to support their information systems.

Further information on testing can be found in the IT Infrastructure Library volume: *Testing an IT Service for Operational Use* and in the Information Systems Engineering Library volume: *Management of Software Maintenance*.

4.6 Documentation

The CCTA study showed that software system maintainers found documentation at program level is the most important feature of useful documentation, closely followed by system specifications and structure diagrams.

Maintainers use the documentation for live systems to solve problems quickly, to understand users' new requirements and to identify and design solutions. The development team must carefully consider the requirements of the maintainers themselves, who must be able to:

- understand what the system does

- identify system components

- identify system interfaces

- identify system limits and capacities

- trace through progressive levels of detail the requirements, design and code of software

- understand what each program does

- navigate data flows
- navigate execution paths
- cross-reference programs and data.

In order to provide maintainers with the maximum help, documentation should be:

- hierarchical
- structured
- produced to agreed and understood installation standards. (If these standards do not exist, then appropriate installation standards should be prepared and used.)
- cross-referenced
- succinct
- available to all IT personnel
- automated and available on line.

Documentation should be complete, consistent and up to date: if the development team cannot guarantee this, the documentation has little value to the maintainer or even to the developers themselves, who may well have to apply changes and corrections to the code prior to full implementation. Documentation should, therefore, be produced and maintained to meet maintainers' requirements, and should be managed through change control, configuration management and quality assurance procedures. Documentation should be tested as part of the testing process and accepted, via 'sign off', by the maintainers as acceptable for their purposes.

It is, of course, essential to fully document maintenance changes themselves, using the same standards as developers. The actual contents of the documents supplied by the developers to the maintainers will vary.

However, program level documentation should always include:

- change history and configuration details
- program description and purpose
- context diagrams
- data descriptions
- process descriptions, including those for common modules and error processing
- design and implementation documents, including structure charts, module hierarchy charts and cross references
- limits and volumes for data and processes.

At the system level, the key elements contained in documentation include:

- change history and configuration details
- description and purpose
- data model descriptions and dictionary
- logical process model
- physical process model, including security and controls, and transaction descriptions and profiles
- limits and volumes.

Developers must consider maintainers' needs and must include documentation of any development utilities and testing facilities. Because developers use these tools frequently and see them as 'one-off' tools, instructions for their use tend to be overlooked and their documentation forgotten. This must not be allowed to happen.

Chapter 4
Developing maintainable software systems

4.7 Adherence to standards and methods

Software systems benefit from the use of consistent installation standards and methods. The extent of the take-up of the standards and methods is as important as the standards themselves. There are three different scenarios:

1. there are no standards or methods: each person working to their own set of standards

2. there are standards and methods, but they are not always adhered to

3. standards and methods are adhered to.

Clearly, situation 3 is the most desirable state of affairs for maintainability. Situation 2 is perhaps the worst case because maintainers, expecting a standard approach, find it harder to maintain non-standard code. Other system elements, such as documentation, are similarly affected.

SSADM, PRINCE and CRAMM provide an interlinked set of standard methods developed by CCTA.

4.8 Maintainability and quality

Maintainability is one measure of the quality of a developed system. Progress checks should be built into the quality control process to monitor maintainability throughout development. Members of the maintenance team, project reviewers, quality inspectors and auditors should be involved in the assessment of maintainability. Maintainability should be measured for the post implementation review (and monitored thereafter) using the techniques described in Chapter 6.

Adherence by the organisation's IS providers in general, and the software developers and maintainers in particular, to the requirements of the international quality management standard ISO 9001 will add quality to the development and maintenance tasks, and will contribute to ensuring good maintainability of software systems. Some guidance on this topic is available in the Information Systems Engineering Library volume: *Quality Management for PRINCE and SSADM Projects*.

5 Preserving and improving the maintainability of software

5.1 Introduction

Application software systems have to be amended to correct errors and to implement changes necessary to keep the software system in line with changing business requirements. However, it is the implementation of these amendments which can gradually destroy any useful structure the software system may have had, and this contributes to poor software maintainability. A system which already has poor maintainability characteristics will be more hazardous to amend, with consequent increased time and cost required for the work, and an increased risk of introducing further error. This chapter deals with the actions which can be taken during software maintenance to preserve and improve software maintainability.

5.2 Maintainability objectives

Maintainers of software often have little or no control over the state of the systems they inherit. Whether or not a system has been designed with maintainability in mind will often only become apparent when it is necessary to make a change or correct an error. The approach for assessing maintainability described in Chapter 6 and Annexes A and B provides a means of gaining some appreciation of the maintainability of systems at the time they are passed to the software maintenance team. During the maintenance phase, Application software systems should be assessed periodically, or after a block of maintenance work, in order to indicate the extent of any change in the maintainability of the software and provide a benchmark for future reference. These assessments will also provide information to enable the maintenance team determine what steps, if any, need to be taken to improve maintainability.

Once a software system has been passed to the maintenance team it is then their responsibility to ensure that where software maintainability is inherently good it is safeguarded, and where it is poor it is improved. Steps taken to improve software maintainability will be beneficial when making future amendments. It is worth remembering that the next maintainer has to build on the current work, so this should be carried out to the highest standards.

Chapter 4 has already covered a range of factors which affect software maintainability. Many of these factors, plus others, will be applicable during the maintenance phase of the life of the software system.

Maintainability objectives can be set for existing systems as well as for those under development. The aim is to improve the software, the ease and reliability of carrying out necessary amendments and the consequent responsiveness to business change.

Because software maintenance covers a wide range of activity, the issues to be considered are dealt with by reference to the four major categories of maintenance, which are:

- corrective maintenance (correction of processing, performance or implementation failures in application software)

- perfective maintenance (any modification or enhancement of the existing functionality of application software)

- adaptive maintenance (changes made to application software to adapt it for a change in the supporting environment, network or hardware platform)

- preventive maintenance (action taken to make subsequent maintenance of application software more efficient and reliable).

Chapter 5
Preserving and improving the maintainability of software

5.3 Corrective maintenance

The central concern of corrective maintenance is to:

- identify the origin and cause of the error
- determine the solution
- implement the solution.

Speed is often of the essence for corrective maintenance in order that system operation can be restored quickly.

Where circumvention is applied to provide a quick 'fix', the error must be properly corrected later. All work must be fully documented and amendments to the code must not destroy its structure.

Where there is documentation showing the structure of the software system, the amendment should be made by modifying this and then amending the code as appropriate. In these circumstances, amending the code without reference to the design documentation will not only worsen the structure of the software, but will leave the documentation out of step with the code. If this approach continues, the documentation will quickly become of little value. Worse still, if subsequent maintenance work is then carried out based on the documented structures, the resultant changes will almost certainly cause fresh errors to occur which may prove difficult to trace and correct. Where standards are in place for development and/or maintenance, these must be adhered to.

The maintainer has the following requirements:

- access to accurate and complete documentation to navigate data and processing paths and so to assess quickly the impact of the error on the system's operation and availability

- technical environment facilities to aid dynamic debugging and editing and to restore the system

- test facilities in which to simulate the live problem and to test the solution.

The environmental facilities required are as follows:

- editing and debugging tools

- recovery/restart facilities for the system

- the ability to replicate the live system or problem (ideally in the test environment)

- JCL tools to create/amend JCL quickly (where appropriate)

- tools for impact analysis (to assess quickly and accurately the effect of the error and limit any damage).

Impact analysis is best performed with support tools to search code, together with automated features such as repositories and data dictionaries. Automated documentation can be particularly useful to check cross-references between system components.

5.4	**Perfective maintenance**	Perfective maintenance should be managed through the organisation's change control procedures and, where appropriate, project management procedures (see Figure 2, section 3.3). Perfective maintenance covers all enhancements to a software system and all other changes needed to keep the software in line with changes in the business requirement. Typically it accounts for around 60% of the total maintenance effort, and as this work is often similar to development work, it offers the greatest opportunity to maintainers to affect the maintainability of a software system.

Chapter 5
Preserving and improving the maintainability of software

All work must be carried out in accordance with the organisation's procedural and technical standards. In particular, where methods such as SSADM and SDM have been used in the initial analysis and design of a software system, it is essential that these methods continue to be used during maintenance. Even where these methods have been introduced into the organisation subsequent to the original development, perfective maintenance offers an ideal opportunity to apply them to existing software, and in this way the overall quality and maintainability of the software will be improved.

System enhancements introduce a risk to the software's maintainability unless assessed, controlled, tested and implemented effectively. Testing is particularly important because it reduces the risk of introducing new errors which will have to be corrected.

Rather than implementing changes piecemeal, it is better to batch them into releases. This reduces risk by lowering the frequency of change into the workplace. It also optimises testing and implementation effort and the cost of redocumentation and retraining. The timing and content of each release depends on business priorities, other changes to the same programs or other interfacing systems and the costs and benefits of the timing of the changes involved.

All changes must be fully documented with particular reference to program-level documentation and structure diagrams. Where difficulty was experienced in carrying out accurate impact analysis or in making a change because of the quality or lack of existing documentation, the opportunity should be taken to improve or create this in order to assist future maintainers.

Perfective maintenance may be minimised by adding functionality to the software system which allows users more flexibility. Report generators are a good example as they allow users to customise output which is subject to frequent change. However, there can be significant disadvantages in this approach if it is applied inappropriately or without adequate user training. For example, it could contribute to hardware overload at peak times. Furthermore, the use of such tools is rarely tested by the users and they may generate incorrect results without realising the fact, or waste time making mistakes. These factors must be considered when proposing such flexibility.

Users are often surprised at the difficulty of making changes to software. Good working relationships between system users and maintainers will have a major impact on the overall maintainability of a software system. If there is a proper two-way flow of information at appropriate times, this will help to reduce misunderstandings and make all concerned aware of the problems and benefits involved in making changes to the software. User involvement in the analysis of the impact of requested changes will:

- help to ensure that this work is carried out more effectively

- lessen the risk of unexpected effects on the human/computer interface

- reduce the risk of having to make further changes or corrections in the future.

Indeed, with a better appreciation of the users' requirements, the maintainers may be able to offer constructive suggestions as to the inclusion of additional facilities in the software which may avoid the need for subsequent change.

Chapter 5
Preserving and improving the maintainability of software

5.5 Adaptive maintenance

Adaptive maintenance does not usually have a significant effect on maintainability, though the need for changes to the application programs cannot be ruled out totally. Nonetheless, the ease of adaptive maintenance can be affected by development decisions and software system factors. If portability is a requirement, it can be improved during maintenance by ensuring that the software system conforms to good industry-wide standards. For example, the use of language compilers which conform to the appropriate ISO standard will contribute to portability. Improving portability is unlikely to yield other long-term maintainability benefits. However, the process of adaptive maintenance offers an opportunity to carry out preventive maintenance to improve post-adaptation maintainability (see also section 4.3).

5.6 Preventive maintenance

Preventive maintenance offers the most direct approach to improving maintainability. Once an organisation has assessed the maintainability of the software systems it requires, it will then be in a position to decide which systems are most in need of attention, and what action would have the most impact on improving maintainability. Because of the usual high level of perfective and corrective maintenance, there is often little or no resource available for preventive maintenance. However, in view of the savings which can be achieved during maintenance if the maintainability of the software is improved, managers should give serious attention to allocating resources to well-directed preventive maintenance as this will improve the overall productivity of the maintenance team in the future.

The most important areas of preventive maintenance are:

- improving modularity, parameterisation, coupling and cohesion

- improving documentation, especially that which will aid navigability and impact analysis. Annotating code and recording design features will also prove beneficial

- use of reverse engineering tools to produce documentation of the application and system

- improving standardisation across the system or systems.

Preventive maintenance is most likely to be needed for software that was written before the adoption of standards and methods for software development and maintenance.

The maintenance team manager should pay close attention to naming conventions, structure and modularity and language conventions. Preventive maintenance must be targeted on software systems which are important to the organisation and which have a high level of change or problem traffic. Much preventive maintenance is simple and can be tackled during perfective or adaptive maintenance.

5.7 Maintenance staff

There are links between the maintainability of software systems and:

- the maintenance team's interpersonal skills

- the pressure the team feels itself to be under

- the team's perception of management commitment to maintenance.

5.7.1 Interpersonal skills

A maintainer has to communicate with many people, including the manager, other team members, other IT services and development groups, users and their managers. Additionally, the maintainer may need to deal with vendors of software and hardware. The maintainer therefore needs:

- technical proficiency

- problem solving skills

- communication skills, such as the ability to listen and give clear instructions

- personal skills, such as the ability to adapt to changing circumstances, assertiveness and empathy

- business knowledge and the ability to discuss issues with the users in terms which they can understand.

Many of these skills can be taught and incorporated into personal development and training programmes. The accumulated knowledge and experience of the team can be written up and held in a repository. If this is well indexed it will provide new members of the team with easy access to necessary information.

5.7.2 Pressure

Too much pressure can adversely affect maintainability. Managers must ensure that the workload stretches the team and makes demands on them without being unduly excessive. Without realistic targets to aim for, the team will lose drive. On the other hand, excessive pressure makes it hard to achieve good quality results. A key problem is that work of high priority must take precedence over work in progress which is of less importance. Remedies include:

- re-organising the team so that a separate section handles corrective maintenance

- dissuading users from changing the priorities of perfective maintenance once they have been approved, except through the appropriate change procedures.

5.7.3 Management commitment

Management commitment is closely linked to pressure. Excessive pressure may arise simply because the team is under-resourced. Management commitment to the maintenance task is essential to ensure that the maintenance team is adequately staffed, motivated and productive. To achieve these objectives, it may be necessary for management to reduce or re-schedule the workload, supplement the resources or perhaps invest in equipment and/or software tools. Members of the maintenance team must perceive that there is a high level of commitment from management in order that their own motivation is affected. The team must feel that the work they do is valued and has importance. The manager must therefore:

- set realistic, achievable goals

- organise effectively and equip adequately

- recognise and acknowledge achievement.

6 Monitoring software maintainability

6.1 The need to measure

The maintainability of a software system should be monitored throughout the life of the system, to identify any improvement or deterioration which may have occurred. In order to do this, the main factors affecting maintainability need to be measured periodically, perhaps every six months, or after a particular set of amendments have been implemented. Measurement needs to be applied in the same way each time. If a standard approach is followed by an organisation for all its software systems, comparison between systems may be made which will provide assistance in setting business priorities for maintenance and for any remedial action which may be thought necessary.

The Information Systems Engineering Library volume *Management of Software Maintenance* offers guidance on evaluating the overall effectiveness of a software system, and this chapter, used in conjunction with Annexes A and B, provides an approach for assessing the maintainability of software. It can be applied to both new and existing systems and the results obtained will highlight any areas which may be adversely affecting maintainability or even inhibiting system maintenance.

Annexes A and B provide a means of gathering data about a system, while this chapter gives information on the approach itself and how the results obtained should be interpreted. The approach described can be tailored to the individual requirements of an organisation.

6.2 Assessing software maintainability

Two ways of assessing software maintainability are provided. Every software system has individual factors which have an effect on its ease of maintenance and these are assessed to provide the Maintainability Measure (MM). The productivity and quality of the maintenance work carried out are assessed to provide the Maintainability Index (MI). The MM and MI each provide information about the software system. However, the most value is obtained when they are used together as recommended here.

The MM information is best compiled by a team leader or senior member of the maintenance team. Some of the measures may not be easy to assess and it is helpful to have a practical knowledge of the systems being supported. Where it is not easy to obtain an exact measurement, an estimate will suffice; it is more important to complete the assessment than to abandon it for lack of precision. The MI information will have to be compiled by reference to both the IS service providers and the business customers of the application software system.

Results from the two sets of data should be combined in a two-dimensional diagram to give an assessment of a software system's maintainability. If MI cannot be calculated because a system has been frozen or only requires infrequent amendment, MM can still be measured. It provides useful information on which to base action for improving maintainability.

Where distributed systems are being considered, and identical software is not installed at all locations, it may be helpful to regard these as separate sub-systems.

Chapter 6
Monitoring software maintainability

6.2.1 Maintainability Measure

The factors affecting the MM vary widely in their importance. Some, such as documentation, have a very large impact; others less so. Factors are, therefore, weighted. The factors themselves may consist of several features, each making a contribution to the factor. These features may also differ in their relative importance.

A score sheet for the MM is provided in Annex A together with guidance for scoring and instructions for completing the form. Organisations may chose to modify these factors or add others to meet their particular circumstances. However, if different factors or features are used for different software systems, this will detract from any cross system comparison which is one of the benefits of applying the approach.

6.2.2 Maintainability Index

The MI is the second aspect of measuring maintainability. It measures:

- *error resolution time* (the time taken to correct or resolve an error)

- *resolution result* (the effect of the correction)

- *change time* (the time taken to implement a planned system change or enhancement)

- *change result* (the effect of the change).

These statistics provide information on the productivity (time taken) and quality (effect of implementation) of the current maintenance work. MI is used initially to assess current performance and provides a simple ongoing measure to monitor future performance.

A score sheet for the MI is provided in Annex B together with instructions for completing the form.

6.3 Assessment results

6.3.1 Interpretation of the results

The above approach provides a relatively simple and effective means of obtaining information on maintainability of application software systems. The approach offers a means of comparing the maintainability of two or more systems and comparing the maintainability of a given system over time.

However, because of the subjectivity involved in scoring some of the features assessed in determining MM and MI, it is not realistic to compare systems between different organisations where different subjectivity will have been applied. Such comparisons are further invalidated if organisations have modified the factors or features used in compiling MM.

When evaluating the results of the assessment exercise, it is not helpful merely to look at the end figures produced for either MM or MI. The same number could be achieved for two systems, but the individual elements which contributed to that number could be very different from one another and hence the systems would require different remedial action.

The results must, therefore, be interpreted intelligently if true benefit is to be derived. There are no 'magic numbers' to aim for. Wisely used, however, the information derived will be of considerable value to the software maintainers and business alike.

Chapter 6
Monitoring software maintainability

6.3.2 Evaluation of the Results

Once the results for maintainability measure and maintainability index are obtained for the application software systems of interest to the organisation, points should be plotted in a graph as shown in Figure 4. In both cases, a high score indicates poor maintainability.

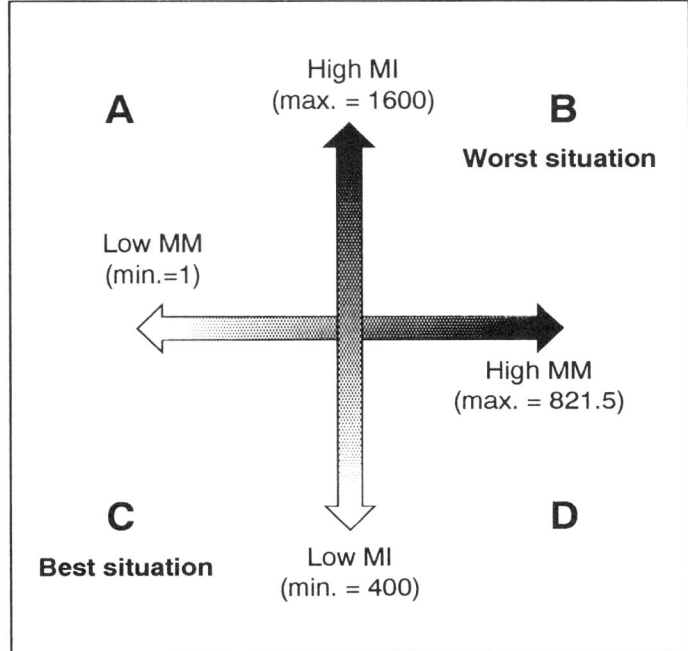

Figure 4: Maintainability plot

The point where the axes intersect is variable. It can be fixed for a given organisation by calculating MM and MI for all systems and taking the mean value of each. Systems can then be placed in the appropriate quadrant, depending on their MM and MI scores.

Systems in quadrant C have both a good MI and a good MM. No action is required at the moment, but future measurements should be monitored for any signs of movement towards the other quadrants.

Systems in quadrant A have a poor MI and a good MM. This result may occur when the maintenance team is severely under-resourced or when the maintenance team is unfamiliar with a system.

Systems in quadrant D have a poor MM and a good MI. Such systems have a potential maintainability problem, but immediate action is probably not required. A system supported by an experienced team that knows the system well could fall into this quadrant. If key members leave, however, the system could move into quadrant B and, therefore, preventive action may be appropriate.

Systems in quadrant B have a poor MM and a poor MI. These should be given the highest priority for action.

6.4	**Objectives and actions**

Once the systems in most need of attention have been identified, the next step is to determine which are of the greatest importance to the organisation. If the maintainers do not have a clear list of priority systems, it would be helpful to compile one in consultation with business managers. IS staff must not prioritise systems solely from their own viewpoint. When it has been agreed which systems should receive attention, the task of identifying necessary improvements begins. It is important to identify where to start and how to decide which actions will produce the most cost-effective results.

An understanding of where most software maintenance effort is expended is helpful when trying to determine the relative impact of the various maintainability factors. Many organisations do not record their software maintenance effort in sufficient detail to see which activities take up most of the maintainers' time. Annex D lists the five software maintenance steps and it would be useful to determine which step occupies most of the maintenance team's effort and thus incurs the greatest cost. If this information is unavailable, all maintenance staff will need to record accurately their activity over a given period. This period should be long enough to encompass all five steps for both problem solving, and developing and implementing a system enhancement. In addition, when agreeing the period, attention must be given to known peaks or troughs in business-driven activity.

Chapter 6
Monitoring software maintainability

Annex D also contains two tables which show the factors that most affect the five maintenance steps. The tables may be useful when prioritising an action plan to improve maintainability. For example, if the maintainers spend 80% of their time in testing system changes, this area should be addressed first. The tables show that eight significant factors have an impact on testing. If these factors are checked against the maintainability assessment results and ranked according to their scores, this will indicate the actions which will have the greatest beneficial impact on maintainability.

An alternative approach would be to look at the highest scoring features on the MM form, these will provide an indication of the areas most in need of attention. For example, 'no problem management system' (PMS) may have scored the maximum of 16 and 'no test documentation' may have scored the maximum of 7.5. System maintainability would, therefore, be improved more by introducing a PMS than by producing test documentation. Once in place the PMS would benefit all systems under maintenance, with consequent improvements in the maintainability of the organisation's application software. However, test documentation must not be ignored, and may in fact be easiest to improve for that system. Deciding on appropriate objectives will, therefore, depend on understanding the maintainability of systems, the benefits achievable and the availability of resources to carry out changes.

Other software maintenance activities, such as overnight call outs and help desk queries, should be checked to see if they scored badly. Cost reductions in areas such as these can easily justify the cost of writing or updating a user guide or producing clearer operating instructions. Further investigation will be worthwhile; for example, to determine the types of help desk calls.

A maintainability plan should be produced (examples are given in Annex C). It should contain objectives, key tasks and measurements of success.

6.5 Reaping the benefits

Planning, designing and building maintainable software systems improves the effectiveness of IT resources. It results in systems which:

- are easier and quicker to change
- are less error prone
- have longer life-times.

For the business, this means:

- reduced risk
- better value for money
- an improved return on investment.

Of equal importance, maintenance staff will spend less time worrying about the software system itself and have more time to devote to meeting other needs of the business.

Annex A: Maintainability measure

This Annex describes how to measure the significant factors grouped under maintainability measure (MM). Each factor is defined and guidance for scoring the associated features is given in sections A.2 - A.21.

An example of a completed form is provided in A.22.

The list of factors covers the main aspects that affect software maintainability. However, if it is desired to include additional factors or features, this may be done. To avoid inadvertent distortion of the end results care will be needed in arriving at the appropriate scoring or weighting of any additional factors.

A.1 Derivation

Derive the Maintainability Measure (MM) using the form given below. Complete the form as follows:

1 Assess each feature individually. Technical Size, Age and Maintainers' Perception have one score only. For all other factors each feature has a maximum score associated with it which represents the worst case for maintainability.

Only one score is applied for a feature; scores are not added together where several scoring reasons are given for a feature.

For example, in A.16, if there is no testbed available for testing live system changes, the testbed feature scores 3. If there is a testbed of sorts, but imperfect or containing correct data only, allocate a score of 2. If some erroneous data is present and the system is tested fairly thoroughly, score 1. A comprehensive, well-maintained test bed scores 0.

Sections A.2 to A.21 describe each feature and indicate the appropriate score or give guidance for its derivation. Scores may include a decimal point, so long as they fall within the range zero to maximum. Some features require a qualitative judgement; try to make the assessment as objective as possible

2 Each feature score is multiplied by the factor weight to give a weighted score. When all the features for a factor have been assessed, add up the weighted and unweighted scores to give factor totals. The maximum unweighted score for any factor is 10

3 Work through all the factors. When all measurements are completed, add up the weighted totals for the entire list of factors. The lower the overall total, the better the Maintainability Measure. Factors relating to development will remain constant throughout the life of a software system. These factors will need to be assessed the first time MM is used for a software system, but thereafter the figures may be reused without repeating the assessment.

When both the MM and MI have been derived, return to section 6.3 for interpretation of the results.

Annex A
Maintainability measure

Maintainability Factor Assessment Form

Factors	Features			Max Score	Feature Score	Weighted Score
Technical size	2GL	3GL	Mark 2 Func. Points	Weight = 3		
	<700	<1000	<10	0		
	700-1000	1000-2000	11-20	2		
	1001-2000	2001-5000	21-50	3		
	>2000	>5000	>50	5		
	Factor total:					
Complexity				Weight = 9		
	Business requirement			2.5		
	Application			0.5		
	Data structures			1.5		
	Several languages used			1.5		
	Code complexity			2.0		
	Distributed site			0.5		
	Customised software			1.5		
	Factor total:					
Structuredness				Weight = 6		
	Modularity			5		
	Parameterisation			5		
	Factor total:					
Age				Weight = 1		
	<2			10		
	>2			1		
	>4			2		
	>6			3		
	>8			4		
	>10			5		
	>12			6		
	>13			7		
	>14			8		
	>15			9		
	>20			10		
	Factor total:					

Factors	Features	Max Score	Feature Score	Weighted Score
Program and system documentation		Weight =10		
	Narrative description	3		
	Program structure	3		
	System structure	2.5		
	System description/purpose	1.5		
	Factor total:			
Documentation		Weight = 6		
	Up to date/change history	2		
	Available/used daily	1		
	Automated	1		
	Business/application overview	1		
	Navigation aids	2		
	Impact analysis aids	1		
	Annotated code	2		
	Factor total:			
Development process		Weight = 1		
	User contribution to development	5		
	Maintainability as a development objective	3		
	Development standards and methods	2		
	Factor total:			
Development team		Weight = 1		
	Technical skills	2		
	Development experience	3		
	Business knowledge	2		
	Attitude and motivation	3		
	Factor total:			
Development timescale		Weight = 1		
	Tight	5		
	Broken or non-contiguous	5		
	Factor total:			
Development relationships		Weight = 1		
	Customer/developers	2		
	Customer/operations	1		
	Developers/operations	2		
	Developers/technical supporters	2		
	Between customers	2		
	Third party	1		
	Factor total:			

Annex A
Maintainability measure

Factors	Features	Max Score	Feature Score	Weighted Score
Business change traffic		Weight = 2		
	Growing backlog	5		
	No statistics kept	1		
	Frequent releases	4		
	Factor total:			
Problem change traffic		Weight = 3		
	Errors arising from system change	3		
	Growing number of problems	4		
	Stable number of problems	1.5		
	Reducing number of problems	1		
	No statistics kept	0.5		
	Factor total:			
Operating procedures		Weight = 2		
	Uncontrolled releases	2		
	Operations guide	8		
	Factor total:			
Maintenance procedures		Weight = 8		
	Change management	2		
	Problem management	2		
	Release control/configuration management	2		
	Quality management	2		
	Formalised testing procedures	2		
	Factor total:			
Test facilities		Weight = 5		
	Comprehensive testbed	3		
	Test harness	3		
	Documentation	1.5		
	Test tools	1.5		
	Independent test function	1		
	Factor total:			
System users/ customers		Weight = 3		
	Computer literacy	3		
	User guide	6		
	Multiple departments	1		
	Factor total:			

Factors	Features	Max Score	Feature Score	Weighted Score
Maintenance team		Weight = 9		
	Interpersonal skills	3		
	Pressure	0.5		
	Perception of management commitment	2		
	Team attitude to support work	2		
	Team business knowledge	1		
	Technical skills	0.5		
	Experience of languages	0.5		
	Separate planned enhancements	0.5		
	Factor total:			
Maintenance relationships		Weight = 4		
	Customer/maintainers	3		
	Customer/operations	2		
	Maintainers/operations	3		
	Between customers	0.5		
	Third party	1.5		
	Factor total:			
Environmental facilities		Weight = 8		
	Ability to simulate live problems	1.5		
	Live data access	1.5		
	Editor	1.5		
	Debugging tools	1		
	Response times	0.5		
	Backup/recovery	1		
	Tools for impact analysis	1		
	Capacity/performance problems	0.5		
	Job control language	1.5		
	Factor total:			
Maintainers' perception	Average score of team members	Weight = 1 10		

MAINTAINABILITY MEASURE in the range 1 - 821.5

Annex A
Maintainability measure

A.2 Technical size

Definition: The average component size in terms of software, code modules and data structures. The larger the component, the more difficult the system is to maintain.

Score: Apply a single score as outlined below:

Use the average number of lines of code (LOC), excluding comment lines, for 2GL or 3GL code. Take an average from all executable programs including COPYBOOK or INCLUDED code.

In the case of some 4GLs, technical size may not be appropriately assessed on source code, for example where screens are used to access program code held on a database. 4GLs should be scored 2.5 unless mark 2 function point counts are available.

Although function points do not give quite the same measure of size as lines of code, the figures in the table below, based on an average conversion factor for a typical 3GL, are sufficient for the Maintainability Measure if LOC are inappropriate, as for 4GLs, or more difficult to obtain.

Use the table below for lines of code with 2GLs, 3GLs and mark 2 function points.

2GL	3GL	Mark 2 function points	Score
<700	<1000	<10	0
700-1000	1000-2000	11-20	2
1001-2000	2001-5000	21-50	3
>2000	>5000	>50	5

Improving the Maintainability of Software

A.3 Complexity

Definition: This covers the complexity of both the business requirement and the technical solution. The complexity of the system in terms of business functionality will impact the technical solution. Alternatively, complexity can arise solely from a mixed technical platform.

Score:
- a simple *business requirement* such as a straightforward reporting system, scores 0. A complex business requirement such as processing insurer's actuarial tables scores the maximum of 2.5

- a complex *application* containing difficult algorithms, or with interfaces to more than two other systems scores a maximum of 0.5, otherwise 0

- complicated *data structures*, for example one with logical and physical views of a database, scores a maximum of 1.5. Non-hierarchical structures also score 1.5. A hierarchy with three or more levels scores 1.5; one with two levels scores 1. Flat files interlinked by key fields score 0.5 and unlinked files score 0

- a system written in *several languages* scores a maximum of 1.5. A single programming language used with a single transaction processor such as COBOL/TPMS or a single programming language with a database access language, such as ADABAS/NATURAL, scores 1

Annex A
Maintainability measure

- *code complexity* should be formally assessed for the whole system. Wherever possible use an approved algorithm such as Halstead's Difficulty metric, which is based on the use of variables, or McCabe's Cyclomatic Complexity, which measures the number of paths through a piece of code. Several Computer Aided Support and Maintenance tools use a known complexity measure and so may be of help. Any measure used produces a result in the range specific to that measure. Convert the result, by proportion, to the range 0 to 2

- score 0.5 for *distributed sites* or *networked system* and 0 for central or one-site system

- score a maximum of 1.5 for any *customisation* of software package or system software. Score 0 for no customisation.

A.4 Structuredness

Definition: The features of the design and code which indicate a pattern of organisation of its independent parts. Increased structuredness improves the maintainability of the system.

Score: There are two significant features of system structuredness:

- *modularity*
- *parameterisation*.

Score a maximum of 5 for each.

Modularity measures the effect of the removal of repetitive program code and limiting module size. Module size is covered by the Technical Size factor and can be ignored at this stage. One aim is to achieve independence of function, with each module covering processing related to one function, not portions of several; to accomplish this, other modules may be called in a hierarchy. Each module should be similarly structured.

The following measurement reflects the effectiveness of the system's modularity by examining the number of times modules are used. The greater the ratio of number of calls to the number of modules, the greater independence of function exists.

The number of *module* calls in the whole system must be assessed; this count must not include call statements, such as database calls, but only calls to other modules. The following formula gives the modularity feature score:

$$5 \times \frac{(number\ of\ modules - 1)}{number\ of\ module\ calls}$$

The maximum score is 5. If there is a high degree of modularity of non-common code this could adversely distort the figure, and it should be reduced accordingly.

Parameterisation measures the extent to which a system function can be varied without the need for software change.

Score 0 to 5 depending on the extent to which useful parameterisation has been incorporated into the system.

Annex A
Maintainability measure

A.5 Age

Definition: The number of years since the oldest part of the system was partially or fully implemented. A system is likely to become less maintainable once it has reached old age; a very young system will also require more effort to maintain it as faults are detected once the system becomes live.

The age remains the same, even if a substantial portion is redeveloped. In this case, however, you may wish to assess the maintainability of the two subsystems separately. In view of the relatively low importance of age as a maintainability factor, this separation is generally unnecessary. Other factors are more likely to be significant and are more easily addressed.

Score: Apply a single figure between 1 and 10 according to the age of the system.

A.6 Program and software system documentation

Definition: In the terms of this factor, program documentation consists of a narrative description of the program function and a program structure chart or equivalent. Software system documentation consists of system structure specification and system description/purpose.

Score:
- where narrative description is non-existent, out of date or misleading, score a maximum of 3

- where the program structure is non-existent, out of date or misleading, score a maximum of 3

- if there is no system structure documented, score a maximum of 2.5

- if the system description/purpose is available but of doubtful quality and currency, score a maximum of 1.5.

A.7 Other documentation

Definition: Many documents other than those in A.6 may be available, often depending on the system development standards or methodology used, but only those mentioned below were highlighted in the CCTA study as affecting system maintainability.

Score:
- documentation should be *up to date* and is most useful where the document change history is also present. If neither is certain, score 2

- if system documents are neither easily *available* to the maintainers nor used on a frequent basis, score 1

- documentation is often *automated* or partially automated in recently developed systems. This helps to keep it up to date and thus enhances its effectiveness in improving maintainability. If nothing is automated, score 1

- an *overview* of the *business application* improves a system's maintainability by improving business impact analysis. Score 0 if a good one exists, 1 if not

- there are specific items of systems documentation which are of particular use to maintainers. These consist of navigation and impact analysis aids. They include such items as dataflow diagrams, data dictionary and cross-references for example job/program, error message/program, record/program, file/job. *Navigation aids* help to find the way around the system and *impact analysis aids* make assessing and estimating change easier. If no such help exists, score 2 for navigation aids and 1 for impact analysis aids

Annex A
Maintainability measure

- well *annotated code* is of considerable help when trying to find program errors or to change program function. Notes are not always helpful when present and a judgement as to the quality of such comments is needed. Score 2 for poor or non-existent ones and 1 for comments of variable standard. Only score 0 if they are invariably helpful.

A.8 Development process

Definition: So far as maintainability is concerned, three significant factors contribute to the development process:

- the customer's involvement throughout the development process

- maintainability as a specific development objective; where it is, delivered systems are recognisably easier to maintain

- clear standards and methods consistently applied throughout the development lifecycle, which facilitates the development of systems which are easier to understand and maintain.

Score: Score each feature as a maximum unless there is evidence that the development team took them into account. It may be difficult to assess the features in retrospect; if so, old systems should have a maximum score.

- occasionally, the system *customer's involvement* is considerable during requirements definition and systems analysis, but diminishes to progress reporting for the remainder of the development. In this case, score 3. A 0 score only applies where involvement includes test planning, attending walkthroughs, inspections or reviews and hands-on acceptance testing

- a *maintainability objective* such as modularisation of common code should be included in the development project plans and reviews. If it was not included, score 3

- standards and methods must be clearly documented and work checked to ensure they are used. If this is not the case, score 2.

A.9 Development team

Definition: Any aspect of the organisation, attitudes or working practices of the development team which has an effect on the maintainability of software systems.

Score:

- the variety and depth of *technical skill* possessed by the developers contributes to the quality and thus maintainability of the delivered system. Unless all team members have at least two years experience of every technical skill required, score 1. Score 2 if only one team member has two years experience in any skill

- if any team member, including the manager, has less than two years experience of *development work*, score 3. If all have two years development experience, but less experience with the development method, such as SSADM or PRINCE, score 1 or 2 according to the proportion of the team with experience. Score 0 if all team members have two years or more development experience with the prescribed methods

- a development team's *business knowledge* contributes to a system's maintainability. If there is none, score 2. Some knowledge would score low providing it is a knowledge of the relevant business function that the system supports. Measurement should be taken across the whole of the development team

- the development team's attitude to development

work is also important. If everyone would rather be working elsewhere, score 3. A team needs to gel to work together effectively. A number of independent people in advisory roles can be tolerated, but if there is no team spirit, score 3.

A.10 Development timescale

Definition: The development project timescale lasts from the start of work on the project plan to the completion of the system's live installation.

Score: An optimum development timescale results in an even distribution of pressure, feasible deadlines, a dedicated team, no need to reallocate tasks or change work and priorities to meet changing business needs.

- a *tight* timescale leads to corners being cut, overlapped tasks, changing priorities and increased pressure. If timescales were not tight, score 0. If there is evidence of a tight development timescale which was well controlled, score 3. Otherwise a tight timescale scores 5

- a *broken* timescale causes loss of vision and drive and may result in loss of team members. Re-work may be required and, unless work is fully documented when suspended, some issues are likely to be lost and not addressed later. Team motivation is at least reduced and confidence is lost. Score 5 if a break lasting more than one month occurred during development. Score 0 if there was no break.

A.11 Development relationships

Definition: The nature of the communication between groups involved with the system development, both within and between the IT and customer departments. Where third party services or products are involved, relationships with the supplier are also relevant.

Score: The more structured the relationships between the groups of people, the smoother the working relationship which results. Easy access between groups avoids assumptions, misinterpretation and in-built errors in the developing systems.

Each feature listed should be scored separately even when the same people are involved. Multiple groups should be assessed on the worst case, for example where maintainers liaised with two groups providing technical support.

All features score maximum points, unless the relationship is ideal and can withstand occasional crises.

A.12 Business change traffic

Definition: The state of the backlog of changes to the system which affects both the morale of the maintenance team and the customers' perception of service. In particular, if the list is growing the system is being inadequately maintained or the backlog is not under control.

Score: The size of the backlog must be measured over a period of at least three months, depending on the nature of the system and business cycles:

- if the *backlog is growing every month*, score 5; if it increased at least once score 3; if there was no increase score 0

- if *no statistics* are kept, score 1. In this case, the backlog growth will have to be ascertained by other means

- *frequent releases* may indicate a lack of thorough testing but may be due to difficulties with business change traffic. Even if another cause is clear make a score here. Emergency releases are included in this count. Releases are frequent if they occur more than once per month, in which case score the maximum of 4. If releases are less often than once per month score 0.

A.13 Problem change traffic

Definition: The backlog and reasons for problems which arise in the live environment. An unstable system is probably one which is becoming unmaintainable. Inadequate testing may well be the cause.

Score:
- if statistics are available, it may be possible to identify *errors caused by a system change*. If any are present, score 3

- the backlog of reported problems must be measured as for business change traffic. A *growing number of problems* scores 4. A *stable number of problems* may still indicate maintenance difficulties if serious problems are not being cleared; score 1.5. Even a *reducing number* is a negative indicator, if some outstanding problems are serious; score 1

- a *lack of statistics* scores 0.5.

A.14 Operating procedures

Definition: The amount of change made to the hardware and systems software which supports the system and the degree of self-sufficiency exercised by the system's operations staff.

Score:
- a good *operations guide* reduces the number of calls to support teams from operations. If there isn't one, score a maximum of 8. If there is a good one which covers all system messages and recovery/restart procedures and it is up to date, score 0. Most operations manuals score between 2 and 6

- for frequent, *uncontrolled upgrades* to packages and systems software, score the maximum of 2. If, however, such upgrades always include system testing, score 1. If the maintainers are not consulted on the impact and scheduling of upgrades, score 0.5; if they are consulted, score 0.

A.15 Maintenance procedures

Definition: Any set of standard procedures or methods followed by an organisation to maintain a system.

Score: Each procedure scores 2 if absent, ill-defined or not used. A thorough, well used procedure scores 0 if used AT ALL TIMES. Use your own judgement if the procedure is incomplete or used sometimes.

Annex A
Maintainability measure

The information Systems Engineering Library volume: *Management of Software Maintenance* and the IT Infrastructure Library volumes listed in the Bibliography cover the relevant maintenance control procedures in more detail.

- *change management* must include change prioritisation processes and appropriate bundling of system changes; if not raise the score

- a busy help desk may be an indicator of a failure of *problem management*. Full problem management procedures will deal with problems on the basis of severity and may require that little effort is spent on enquiries or problems of low severity (these can be dealt with only as an incidental part of a future release)

- *release control*, including *effective configuration management*, is vital to preserving maintainability

- a *quality management system* must include maintenance and quality control must be rigorous. A score should be allocated specifically with maintenance in mind, so a quality management system that applies only to software development scores 2

- the lack of *formalised testing procedures* introduces risk and dependency on individuals' experience of support work. Good testing procedures, resulting from an overall test plan, include test stopping criteria.

A.16 Test facilities

Definition: Any testing facilities including a testbed, test harness, test documentation, test tools and test quality.

Score:
- a *testbed* is a prerequisite for appropriate regression testing and scores 3 if not present
- a *test harness* simplifies the testing process, encourages testbed use and helps eliminate test errors. Score 3 if there is no such facility
- if there is no test *documentation* available, testing tends to be ad hoc and depends on individual expertise; score a maximum of 1.5 for no documentation
- the lack of *test run support tools* can lead to a proliferation of methods for test data creation and result checking within the team. These may be encompassed into a test harness. A lack of tools scores 1.5
- test quality is optimised if undertaken by a *team independent* of the system developers and maintainers. Score 1 if this isn't the case.

A.17 System users/customers

Definition: Any users or purchasers of the system. Where users and customers have a degree of computer literacy, system maintainability is improved.

Score:
- if *computer literacy* is low or non-existent, score 3. If some users have understanding score 2, if all users have some skill, score 1. If all users are computer literate and understand the impact of change, score 0

- a *user guide* has a significantly positive effect on maintainability. It is imperative that it is up to date and easily and widely used; score zero if so and a maximum of 6 if there isn't one. Intermediate scores should be applied depending on the use made of the guide by system users and on its quality

- if a system's users reside in several *different departments* maintainability is adversely affected unless a single co-ordinated contact point for support exists within the customer base. Score 0 if this is the case or if there is only one user department, otherwise score 1.

A.18 Maintenance team

Definition: Any aspect of the organisation, attitudes or working practices of the maintenance team which has an effect on the maintainability of software systems.

Score:
- good *interpersonal skills* between maintainers and system users and among maintainers improve the clarity of reporting, analysis, diagnosis and support. Poor skills across the team score 3

- both too little and too much *pressure* affect maintainability. If the team feels pressure is too much or non-existent score 0.5

- the team's *perception of management commitment* to maintenance is closely linked with the pressure it feels. It is the team's *perception* which is measured here scoring 0 if management is perceived to be aware of the need to commit time, money and people to maintain the system effectively. A score of 2 indicates that management are perceived to have no interest in the maintenance function and prefer to invest resources elsewhere

- the team's *attitude to maintenance work* is also important; if everyone would rather be working on development, score 2. A maintenance team does not gel and work effectively with a number of 'independent' members; everyone needs to be a 'team player', if not score 2

- a team's *business knowledge* contributes to a system's maintainability. If there is none, score 1. Some knowledge would score low providing it is a knowledge of the relevant business function that the system supports. One measure should be taken for the maintenance team as a whole

- the variety of *technical skills* needed by the maintenance team also contributes to maintainability. It is best where all team members have all the required skills but if too many specialist skills are needed this may limit the choice of personnel. If many skills are spread across a small team, score 0.5. Similarly, if all team members need to have a variety of specialist skills, score 0.5 even if the current team all have them

- the team's *experience of the languages used, of the environment and of maintenance work* is significant. If anyone has less than two years' experience in any of the three areas, score 0.5

- if the team structure does not *separate planned system enhancements* from 'fire-fighting', score 0.5.

Annex A
Maintainability measure

A.19 Maintenance relationships

Definition: The nature of the communication between groups involved with system maintenance, both within and between the IT and customer departments. Where third party services or products are involved, relationships with the supplier are also relevant.

Score: The more structured the relationships between the groups of people, the smoother the working relationships which result. Easy access between groups facilitates the maintenance process. Problems are better understood and solutions implemented more quickly. Potential business changes are more properly assessed, estimated and planned.

Each feature listed should be scored separately even when the same people are involved. Multiple groups should be assessed on the worst case, for example where there are several user departments.

All features score maximum unless the relationship is known to function smoothly and agreed communication channels are adhered to. If mutual respect is always present and excessive pressure resisted politely, award a 0 score.

A.20 Environment facilities

Definition: The facilities provided by the operating environment, including access to live data, the ability to simulate or reproduce live problems, reliable backups and JCL, easy to use editors and tools for reliable impact analysis.

Score: In most cases, maximum or 0 scores apply but if some parts of the system are better served than others, award intermediate scores.

- if *live problems* cannot be easily *simulated* or reproduced, score 1.5. Simulation must be easy and quick, as live problems are often urgent. A testbed helps but must be immediately available to the maintainers

- *live data* (not live software) often must be *accessed* either to apply a direct change to circumvent a problem or, in some crises, to delete data. If live data is not accessible, problem resolution may be delayed. Score 1.5 if controlled access is not immediately available to the maintainers

- an *editor* should be quick and easy to use. Experienced maintainers need 'expert mode'. Score 1.5 if a good editor is not available to maintainers at all times

- *debugging tools* speed up the maintenance process and improve a system's maintainability by improving the quality of problem solving. Tools which provide step-by-step execution of a program with on-line displays score 0 here, but the ability to stop program execution and make dumps immediately available is of great help and scores 0.5. Anything less scores 1

- a fast *response time* at the maintainer's terminal for editing changes is needed (for example less than two seconds), together with a fast general response (for example less than four seconds). Anything slower causes frustration and can lead to the maintainer taking larger steps during error correction, instead of the small, confirmed steps that ensure there is no knock-on effect. Score 0.5 unless the above limits are always met

- a system with slow *backup/recovery* processes is more difficult to maintain as it will influence the way in which errors are resolved. It should be possible to restart a system quickly and easily, if this is the case score 0. If any data rekeying is necessary for full recovery, score 1

- *tools for impact analysis* automate and speed up the process of assessing change, improving the quality of the change and preserving system maintainability. Such tools work most effectively with a data dictionary or repository. They may also provide assistance in producing cross references and as navigation aids. Score 0 if a comprehensive tool is available. Score 0.5 if some help is available and 1 if not

- *capacity or performance problems* affecting a system impact its maintainability by influencing the ways in which changes are applied. Score a maximum of 0.5 if a constraint such as disc space limits is affecting maintainers' strategy for making system changes

- some operating environments automatically produce correct *job control language*; if not, score 1.5. This is an area which is prone to error and often subject to frequent change.

A.21 Maintainers' perception of maintainability

Definition: Those who directly apply change to a system have the best perception of its maintainability. They have most awareness of ease of change, helpfulness of tools and the influence of the system's attributes.

Score: The maintenance team should be asked to mark the system out of 10, where 0 is a perfect system and 10 one which cannot be maintained (both impossible scores). It is important to get an average view across the team, preferably asking everyone.

A.22 Example of completed Maintainability Factor Assessment Form

Factors	Features			Max Score	Feature Score	Weighted Score
Technical size	2GL	3GL	Mark 2 Func. Points	Weight = 3	0	
	<700	<1000	<10	0		
	700-1000	1000-2000	11-20	2		
	1001-2000	2001-5000	21-50	3		
	>2000	>5000	>50	5		
	Factor total:				0	0
Complexity				Weight = 9		
	Business requirement			2.5	0	
	Application			0.5	0	
	Data structures			1.5	1.5	13.5
	Several languages used			1.5	1.5	13.5
	Code complexity			2.0	0.5	4.5
	Distributed site			0.5	0.5	4.5
	Customised software			1.5	0	
	Factor total:				4	36
Structuredness				Weight = 6		
	Modularity			5	3	18
	Parameterisation			5	5	30
	Factor total:				8	48
Age				Weight = 1		
	<2			10		
	>2			1	1	
	>4			2		
	>6			3		
	>8			4		
	>10			5		
	>12			6		
	>13			7		
	>14			8		
	>15			9		
	>20			10		
	Factor total:				1	1

Annex A
Maintainability measure

Factors	Features	Max Score	Feature Score	Weighted Score
Program and system documentation		Weight =10		
	Narrative description	3	0	0
	Program structure	3	0	0
	System structure	2.5	2.5	25
	System description/purpose	1.5		
	Factor total:		2.5	25
Documentation		Weight = 6		
	Up to date/change history	2	0	0
	Available/used daily	1	0	0
	Automated	1	1	6
	Business/application overview	1	0	0
	Navigation aids	2	2	12
	Impact analysis aids	1	1	6
	Annotated code	2	0	0
	Factor total:		4	24
Development process		Weight = 1		
	User contribution to development	5	2	
	Maintainability as a development objective	3	1	
	Development standards and methods	2	0	
	Factor total:		3	3
Development team		Weight = 1		
	Technical skills	2	1	
	Development experience	3	1	
	Business knowledge	2	1	
	Attitude and motivation	3	1	
	Factor total:		4	4
Development timescale		Weight = 1		
	Tight	5	0	
	Broken or non-contiguous	5	1	
	Factor total:		1	1
Development relationships		Weight = 1		
	Customer/developers	2	1	
	Customer/operations	1	0	
	Developers/operations	2	1	
	Developers/technical supporters	2	1	
	Between customers	2	1	
	Third party	1	0	
	Factor total:		4	4

Factors	Features	Max Score	Feature Score	Weighted Score
Business change traffic		Weight = 2		
	Growing backlog	5	0	
	No statistics kept	1	0	
	Frequent releases	4	0	
	Factor total:		0	0
Problem change traffic		Weight = 3		
	Errors arising from system change	3	0	
	Growing number of problems	4	0	
	Stable number of problems	1.5	0	
	Reducing number of problems	1	1	
	No statistics kept	0.5	0	
	Factor total:		1	3
Operating procedures		Weight = 2		
	Uncontrolled releases	2	0	
	Operations guide	8	4	8
	Factor total:		4	8
Maintenance procedures		Weight = 8		
	Change management	2	0	
	Problem management	2	0	
	Release control/configuration management	2	0	
	Quality management	2	0	
	Formalised testing procedures	2	2	16
	Factor total:		2	16
Test facilities		Weight = 5		
	Comprehensive testbed	3	1	5
	Test harness	3	3	15
	Documentation	1.5	1.5	7.5
	Test tools	1.5	1.5	7.5
	Independent test function	1	1	5
	Factor total:		8	40
System users/ customers		Weight = 3		
	Computer literacy	3	2	6
	User guide	6	3	9
	Multiple departments	1	1	3
	Factor total:		6	18

Annex A
Maintainability measure

Factors	Features	Max Score	Feature Score	Weighted Score
Maintenance team		Weight = 9		
	Interpersonal skills	3	1	9
	Pressure	0.5	0.5	4.5
	Perception of management commitment	2	0.5	4.5
	Team attitude to support work	2	0	0
	Team business knowledge	1	0.5	4.5
	Technical skills	0.5	0.5	4.5
	Experience of languages	0.5	0.5	4.5
	Separate planned enhancements	0.5	0	0
	Factor total:		3.5	31.5
Maintenance relationships		Weight = 4		
	Customer/maintainers	3	0	0
	Customer/operations	2	1	4
	Maintainers/operations	3	1	4
	Between customers	0.5	0	0
	Third party	1.5	1	4
	Factor total:		3	12
Environmental facilities		Weight = 8		
	Ability to simulate live problems	1.5	0	
	Live data access	1.5	0	
	Editor	1.5	0	
	Debugging tools	1	1	8
	Response times	0.5	0	
	Backup/recovery	1	0	
	Tools for impact analysis	1	1	8
	Capacity/performance problems	0.5	0.5	4
	Job control language	1.5	1.5	12
	Factor total:		4	32
Maintainers' perception	Average score of team members	Weight = 1 10	2	2
MAINTAINABILITY MEASURE in the range 1 - 821.5				308.5

Annex B: Maintainability index

Measure the maintainability index using the form given below.

Error resolution time			
Corrected in:	%	Weight	Score
Less than 2 hours		1	
2 hours - 1 day		2	
1 day - 2 days		3	
2 days or more		4	
	Sub-total A:		

Resolution result			
Resolution:	%	Weight	Score
First time/no knock-on		1	
Problem recurred		4	
Caused a different problem		4	
Not possible or uneconomic		3	
	Sub-total B:		

Change time			
Change effort:	%	Weight	Score
Less than 2 days		1	
2 days - 10 days		2	
10 days - 20 days		2	
20 days or more		3	
	Sub-total C:		

Change result			
Implementation:	%	Weight	Score
Not implemented		3	
First time/no knock-on		1	
Caused a different problem		4	
Bad - backed out		5	
Partial implementation only		2	
OK, but requirement changed		1	
	Sub-total D:		

MAINTAINABILITY INDEX A+B+C+D =
(in the range 400-1600)

Complete the form as follows:

1 Under error resolution time, record the percentage of software errors over the last six months which have taken the following effort (including management) to diagnose, test and implement:

- less than two man hours
- two man hours or more but less than one man day
- one to two man days
- two man days or more

2 Under resolution result, record the percentage of software errors over the last six months which have been completed with the following results:

- error corrected at the first attempt with no knock-on effect
- problem recurs after a previous attempt to fix it
- no recurrence, but the fix results in another problem
- an adequate fix is not possible or economic

3 Under change time, record the percentage of approved change requests (including amendments) over the last six months which have taken the following effort (including management) to specify, code, test and implement:

- less than two man days
- two man days or more but less than 10 man days
- 10 man days or more but less than 20 man days
- 20 man days or more

(This does not include effort to estimate the work involved or assess the impact under change control procedures but any work carried out after approval to proceed with the change should be included)

4 Under change result, record the percentage of change requests over the last six months which have been completed with the following results:

- change not implemented (uneconomic, or design prevents)

- change introduced at first attempt with no knock-on effects

- implemented change results in unexpected problem elsewhere

- knock-on effect so severe that the change was backed out

- change only partially implemented

- change was implemented satisfactorily, but the requirement changed

5 After recording the percentage value for each category, multiply by the weights shown on the form. Add up the scores for each category, then add the four categories together to arrive at the maintainability index. The lower the score the better the software system's maintainability.

When both MI and MM have been calculated, return to Chapter 6 and plot MI against MM. See sections 6.3 and 6.4 for a discussion of the results.

Annex C: Example maintainability plans

The maintainability plan is an approach for setting objectives for maintainability and identifying the technical solutions required to achieve them.

A maintainability plan should be raised at the start of software development and monitored until the software system has completed its post implementation review.

Once the software system has been implemented the maintainability plan should be reviewed and re-issued, as the objectives are likely to be different, and reviewed regularly as part of a service improvement program.

The following items should be included:

Objectives: The resulting impact on maintenance.

Measures of success: A way of measuring that the objective has been achieved. Objectives that cannot be measured should not be included.

Key Activities: Particular tasks which will be undertaken to achieve the objective.

Timetable and Milestones: Plan of action on project plans.

Assumptions: Assumptions and inspections at the time the maintainability plan was produced.

Dependencies: Resources and other implications.

Two brief examples are attached to give ideas of what may be included. Section 4 contains further detail of the issues which could be addressed.

Example A: A system currently being maintained for which a replacement is being developed on a different platform

Objective: The objective of the replacement software system is to reduce current maintenance costs by 40%.

Measure of success: 40% less technical resource while still maintaining current service levels.

Key activities: Analysis of history and trends in requirements for change.

Analysis of problems and their origins.

Incorporate these results into the new design.

Design user enhanceable functions to meet unforeseen change based on trends from the analysis of changes.

Systems testing to address specifically known difficulties; for example, restart/recovery facilities.

Systems tests to be reusable so that they can be used by the ongoing maintenance team.

Timetable and milestones: As project plan.

Assumptions: History of changes and problems is available.

User expectations of future business changes are accurate.

Dependency: Effort from current support team is available to assist with analysis.

Annex C
Example maintainability plans

Example B: A live system with management concerns that too much technical effort is being spent on day to day support. There is a steady increase in the backlog of enhancements.

Objectives: To reduce support effort by 50% within one calendar year and to begin decreasing the backlog of enhancements.

Measures of success: A steady reduction in the Maintainability Measure, Maintainability Index and size of backlog (measured in days effort outstanding).

Key activities: Analyse the support activities using the metrics collected with a view to identifying major areas where effort is expended.

Compare these areas with the Maintainability Measure to identify proactive improvements which will give maximum benefit.

Assess the effort in undertaking this work.

Plan and schedule these activities.

Review the metrics, Maintainability Index and Maintainability Measure monthly.

Timetable and milestones: Plan of action to be available in one month's time.

Assumption: Currently collected metrics include enough detail for analysis.

Dependency: The users accept the inevitable short term increase in the backlog.

89

Annex D: The process and activities of software maintenance

This Annex contains information on the process and activities of software maintenance. It is included for reference when considering the most effective measures required to improve software maintainability. The information below is of course very generalised, but the table may be utilised in deriving action plans following maintainability assessment.

The different steps of maintenance as listed in section 3.3.3 are:

1. understanding the problem or requirement for change

2. identifying and describing the changes to be made to the system

3. making the changes

4. testing the changed software, and regression testing

5. implementing the upgraded system and assessing the entire system at the post implementation review.

In section 3.4 the significant factors were shown in three groups:

- software system
- development process
- maintenance process.

Improving the Maintainability of Software

The impact of software system factors is shown in the following table. Please note that this only references the factors of most importance at each stage. If a factor is not shown at a given stage, this does not necessarily mean that it has no relevance at all. So, for example, the technical size of the system affects the understanding of the problem and the ability to identify the solution. The language used to write the software system, however, has little impact on either of these.

Software System Factors	Understand requirement	Identify Change	Make Change	Test	Implement
Technical size	*	*			
Complexity/ languages	*	*	*	*	*
Structuredness		*	*	*	
Age	*				
Documentation	*	*	*		

Development factors have an impact on all maintenance steps by affecting the overall quality of the software system.

Annex D
The process and activities of software maintenance

The impact of maintenance factors is shown in the following table.

Maintenance Factors	Understand requirement	Identify Change	Make Change	Test	Implement
Problem traffic	*			*	*
Business traffic	*	*			
Technology	*	*			
Maintenance procedures	*		*	*	*
Test facilities				*	
User/customer	*			*	
Maintenance team	*	*	*	*	*
Maintenance relationships	*				*
Environmental facilities	*	*	*	*	*

Bibliography

Information System Guides

The Information System Guides are available from John Wiley & Sons Ltd, Baffins Lane, Chichester PO19 1UD

The following guides are referenced in this publication:

- CCTA IS Guides set A: Management and Planning Set (5 volumes A1-A5)
  ISBN: 0 471 92555 1

- CCTA IS Guides set B: Systems Development Set (8 volumes B1-B8)
  ISBN: 0 471 92556 X

Information Systems Engineering Library

The Information Systems Engineering Library volumes are available from HMSO Books (Dept A), Freepost, Norwich, NR3 1BR, or telephone 071 873 9090, fax 071 873 8200.

The following volumes are referenced by this publication:

- Estimating with Mark II Function Point analysis
  ISBN: 0 11 330578 8

- Management of Software Maintenance
  ISBN: 0 11 330584 2

- Quality Management for PRINCE and SSADM Projects
  ISBN: 0 11 330580 X

IT Infrastructure Library

The IT Infrastructure Library volumes are available from HMSO Books (Dept A), Freepost, Norwich, NR3 1BR, or telephone 071 873 9090, fax 071 873 8200

The following volumes are referenced in this publication:

- Change Management
  ISBN: 0 11 330525 7

- Configuration Management
  ISBN: 0 11 330530 3

- Help Desk
  ISBN: 0 11 330522 2

- Problem Management
  ISBN: 0 11 330527 3

- Service Level Management
  ISBN: 0 11 330521 4

- Software Control and Distribution
  ISBN: 0 11 330537 0

- Software Lifecycle Support
  ISBN: 0 11 330559 1

- Testing an IT Service for Operational Use
  ISBN: 0 11 330560 5

- Third Party and Single Source Maintenance
  ISBN: 0 11 330540 0

Bibliography

Other publications

A Complexity Measure
McCabe
IEEE/Transactions on Software Engineering, 1976

Applied Software Measurement
Capers and Jones
McGraw-Hill, 1991

Controlling Software Projects: Management, Measurement and Estimation
De Marco
Yourdon, 1992

Elements of Software Science
Halstead
Elsevier, 1975

Reverse Engineering: Market Methods and Tools
Evans and Hales
Ovum, 1990

Software Engineering: A Practitioner's Approach
Pressman
McGraw-Hill, 1987

Software Engineering: Metrics and Models
Conte, Dunsmore and Shen
Addison-Wesley, 1986

Software Metrics
Gilb
Winthrop, 1977

Software Metrics: A Rigorous Approach
Fenton
Chapman & Hall, 1991

Software Metrics - Establishing a Company-Wide Programme
Grady and Caswell
Prentice-Hall, 1987

The State of Software Maintenance
Schneidewind
IEEE/Transactions on Software Engineering 1987

Glossary

adaptive maintenance	The change made to application software to adapt it for a change of the supporting environment, or network or hardware platform.
applications	Information systems which support a specific business area.
business case	The financial and management justification for IT proposals.
business change traffic	The number of changes and enhancements made to a software system (perfective maintenance).
CASE	Computer Aided Software Engineering.
CASM	Computer Aided Support and Maintenance.
change control	The evaluation, co-ordination, authorisation (or not) and implementation of changes after formal establishment of their identity and assessment of their impact.
cohesion	A cohesive module performs a single task within a software procedure and requires little interaction with procedures being performed in other parts of a program. Stated simply, a cohesive module should, ideally, do just one thing.
complexity	A measure of the difficulty of following the logical flow of processing through a software system. This may be assessed through use of a set of metrics.
configuration management	The process of identifying and defining the configuration items in a system, recording and reporting the status of configuration items and requests for change, and verifying the completeness and correctness of configuration items.
corrective maintenance	The correction of processing performance or implementation problems in application software.

coupling	A measure of the degree of interdependence between modules.
CCTA risk analysis and management method (CRAMM)	A method which provides a structured and consistent basis to identify and justify all the protective measures necessary to ensure the security of both current and future IT systems used for processing data.
environmental facilities	The facilities provided by the operating environment to the maintainers of software systems.
impact analysis	An examination of the effect of an error, or proposed system change, on the system's operation and on the businesses dependent on it.
installation testing	Testing to find faults in the installed configuration of a software system.
IS	Information Systems.
IT	Information Technology.
job control language (JCL)	A language used to identify a sequence of jobs, describe their requirements to an operating system and control their execution.
logical design	The product of stage 5 of the SSADM software development method.
maintainability	The ease with which software can be corrected when errors or deficiencies occur and can be expanded, modified or contracted to satisfy new requirements.
maintainability index (MI)	One of the two maintainability metrics described in this volume. It is based on productivity and quality of maintenance work.
maintainability measure (MM)	One of the two maintainability metrics described in this volume. It is based on an assessment of the various factors which have an effect on the ease of maintenance of a software system.
maintenance procedures	The procedures used by maintainers to carry out maintenance activities.

Glossary

management plan	A step-by-step forecast of the organisation, resources, activities and end products used to carry out a project. The plan shows the whole project in broad outline and should contain checkpoints at suitable places for monitoring progress, expenditure and other variables.
metric	A quantitative measure of the degree to which a system, component or process possesses a given attribute.
module	A separately compilable piece of software.
modularity	The extent to which a piece of software is designed or structured as a set of highly independent modules.
navigation aids	Documentation charts and other material or software tools that help maintainers to find their way round a software system, also to understand its structure and function.
operating environment	The hardware configuration and the associated systems software and utilities which control and are used by the application software.
package (application)	A set of programs and associated documentation written and distributed to provide a standard solution for a particular business need across a range of organisations or industries.
parameter	A variable, external to program code, which can be changed without the need to make a software change.
parameterisation	A measure of the extent to which a software system has been written incorporating parameters.
perfective maintenance	Any modification or enhancement of the existing functionality or performance of application software.
physical design	The product of Stage 6 of the SSADM software development method
portability	The ease with which a software system can be transferred from one hardware/software configuration to another.

preventive maintenance	Action taken to make subsequent maintenance of application software more efficient and reliable.
PRINCE	A standard method used for project management in government IT departments and other organisations. PRINCE is an acronym for PRojects IN Controlled Environments.
problem traffic	The number of incidents and problems affecting a software system.
regression testing	The testing of an application software system or subsystem following amendment of any part of that software, or of software that might interfere with the application software system, using an agreed set of test cases previously developed to test the existing functionality of the software.
relational data analysis	A technique for deriving data structures which have the least redundant data.
reverse engineering	The process of analysing a software subject to identify the system's components and their interrelationships, and to create representations of the system in another form or at higher levels of abstraction. These representations make the software subject more amenable to enquiry, analysis, re-use, and documentation. Reverse engineering may require the use of a repository, or the generation of information in an appropriate form, and notation for re-engineering into a new system using CASE tools.
SDM	Structured Design Method.
software maintainability	see maintainability.
software maintenance	Any modification of a software product after delivery to correct faults, to improve performance or other attributes or to adapt the product to a changed environment. (IEEE Standard P1219.)

Glossary

structured systems analysis and design method (SSADM)
SSADM is a non-proprietary and publicly available method which provides a structured set of procedural, technical and documentation standards designed specifically for analysing business needs and undertaking software development.

structuredness
The features of a software system's design and code which indicate a pattern of organisation of its independent parts.

supplier
Any provider of bespoke or packaged software or software services.

test harness
A collection of test run support tools, for automating test preparation, execution and maintenance.

test stopping criteria
Methods for determining when to stop testing; more detailed information may be found in the IT Infrastructure Library module *Testing an IT Service for Operational Use*.

tools
Software packages which help the developers or maintainers of software systems to improve the productivity or quality of work.

Printed in the United Kingdom for HMSO
Dd297309 11/93 C7 G3397 10170